Dedication

The entire "Foreign Language Through Fairy Tales" series is dedicated to all the children of the world.

It is through their understanding, appreciation, and celebration of our differences that the world will become a better and safer place for us all.

A few things to remember...

- In this fairy tale, you'll notice that some of the German words have a new letter of the alphabet. It's the letter "ß" which looks a lot like our letter "B," but it's not! It's called an "eszett" which is used to represent "ss." For example:

    foot = **Fuss**, but it's always written as **Fuß**.
    big = **gross**, but it's always written as **groß**.

- You'll notice that in German, all nouns (those words that represent a person, place, or thing) begin with an uppercase letter. That's because in German, ALL nouns are written this way! For example:

    girl=**Mädchen** • house=**Haus** • party=**Fest** • prince=**Prinz**

- The words in *green italics* throughout this fairy tale are words you've already learned in previous levels! Do you still remember what they mean?

1

Tochter →

sehr →

Once upon a time, there was a *Papa* who had an eldest (daughter), Julie, a middle **Tochter**, Tessa, and a youngest **Tochter** named Belle. He loved them (very much). He was getting ready to take

Learn GERMAN Through Fairy Tales

Beauty and the BEAST

Book Design & Production: Slangman Kids *(a division of Slangman Inc. and Slangman Publishing)*

Copy Editor: Julie Bobrick
Illustrated by: "Migs!" Sandoval
Translators: Teut Deese & Petra Wirth
Proofreader: Kai Cofer

Published by: Slangman Kids *(a division of Slangman Inc. and Slangman Publishing)* 12206 Hillslope Street, Studio City, CA 91604 •USA • Toll Free Telephone from USA: 1-877-SLANGMAN (1-877-752-6462) • From outside the USA: 1-818-SLANGMAN (1-818-752-6462) • Worldwide Fax 1-413-647-1589 • Email: info@slangman.com • Website: www.slangman.com

"Migs!" Sandoval
✷ our illustrator ✷

Miguel *"Migs!"* Sandoval has been drawing cartoons since the age of 6 and has worked on numerous national commercials and movies as a sculptor, model builder, and illustrator. He was born in Los Angeles and was raised in a bilingual household, speaking English and Spanish. He currently lives in San Francisco where he is working on his new comic book series!

ISBN10: 1891888-889
ISBN13: 978189888-885
Printed in the U.S.A.

10 9 8 7 6 5 4 3 2 1

Order Form

Preview chapters & shop online!
www.slangman.com

SHIP TO: _____

_____

_____

_____

Contact/Phone/Email: _____

Method of Payment (Check one):

☐ Personal Check or Money Order
(Must be in U.S. funds and drawn on a U.S. bank.)

☐ VISA ☐ Master Card ☐ Discover ☐ American Express ☐ JCB

☐☐☐☐☐☐☐☐☐☐☐☐☐☐☐☐
Credit Card Number

_____ ☐☐ ☐☐
Signature   Expiration Date

QTY	ISBN-13	TITLE	PRICE	LEVEL	TOTAL COST
English to CHINESE (Mandarin)					
	9781891888-793	Cinderella	$14.95	1	
	9781891888-854	Goldilocks	$14.95	2	
	9781891888-915	Beauty and the Beast	$14.95	3	
English to FRENCH					
	9781891888-755	Cinderella	$14.95	1	
	9781891888-816	Goldilocks	$14.95	2	
	9781891888-878	Beauty and the Beast	$14.95	3	
English to GERMAN					
	9781891888-762	Cinderella	$14.95	1	
	9781891888-830	Goldilocks	$14.95	2	
	9781891888-885	Beauty and the Beast	$14.95	3	
English to HEBREW					
	9781891888-922	Cinderella	$14.95	1	
	9781891888-939	Goldilocks	$14.95	2	
	9781891888-946	Beauty and the Beast	$14.95	3	
English to ITALIAN					
	9781891888-779	Cinderella	$14.95	1	
	9781891888-823	Goldilocks	$14.95	2	
	9781891888-892	Beauty and the Beast	$14.95	3	
English to JAPANESE					
	9781891888-786	Cinderella	$14.95	1	
	9781891888-847	Goldilocks	$14.95	2	
	9781891888-908	Beauty and the Beast	$14.95	3	
English to SPANISH					
	9781891888-748	Cinderella	$14.95	1	
	9781891888-809	Goldilocks	$14.95	2	
	9781891888-861	Beauty and the Beast	$14.95	3	
Japanese to ENGLISH 絵本で えいご を学ぼう					
	9781891888-038	Cinderella	$14.95	1	
	9781891888-045	Goldilocks	$14.95	2	
	9781891888-052	Beauty and the Beast	$14.95	3	
Korean to ENGLISH 동화를 통한 ENGLISH 배우기					
	9781891888-076	Cinderella	$14.95	1	
	9781891888-106	Goldilocks	$14.95	2	
	9781891888-113	Beauty and the Beast	$14.95	3	
Spanish to ENGLISH Aprende INGLÉS con cuentos de hadas					
	9781891888-953	Cinderella	$14.95	1	
	9781891888-960	Goldilocks	$14.95	2	
	9781891888-977	Beauty and the Beast	$14.95	3	

Total for Merchandise _____

Sales Tax *(California residents only add applicable sales tax)* _____

Shipping *(See left)* _____

ORDER GRAND TOTAL _____

Prices subject to change

SLANGMAN® KIDS
(a division of Slangman Publishing)

** TO PLACE AN ORDER - CALL, FAX, OR EMAIL: **
Phone: 1-818-752-6462 • Fax: 1-413-647-1589
Email: info@slangman.com • Web: www.slangman.com
12206 Hillslope Street • Studio City, CA 91604

(FORM 07160)

2

a long ⟮trip⟯ and asked each **Tochter**, "What
can I bring you from my **Reise**?" "I'd like a
⟮ring⟯ to wear on my finger," said Julie. "I'd like a
⟮necklace⟯ to wear around my neck." said Tessa.

Reise

Ring

Halskette

3

But Belle, who was the most *hübsch* of all said,

Bitte ← "Please . I don't want a **Ring** to wear on my

finger or a **Halskette** to wear around my neck.

Rose ← All I want is a rose ." He replied, "You shall

4

each receive your [gift]." "Oh, *danke* **sehr**!" said each **Tochter**. Then their *Papa* mounted his [horse] and they shouted, "Have a good **Reise**, *Papa*! We will miss you **sehr**!"

Geschenk

Pferd

As he rode off, each **Tochter** shouted again, "*Auf Wiedersehen, Papa! Auf Wiedersehen!*" until he was out of sight. When it was time for him to return, he first stopped to buy a **Ring** for his eldest

6

Tochter to wear on her finger, a **Halskette** for his second **Tochter** to wear around her neck, but he waited to get closer to his *Haus* to look for a garden where he could find a **Rose** for

Garten

Belle. After a few hours, he saw a magnificent **Garten**. He got off his **Pferd**, walked into the **Garten** and picked a **Rose** that was the most *hübsch* he'd ever seen. At that very *Moment*,

the **Tür** to the **Haus** opened and a [beast] who → **Bestie**

was very **groß** came out and ran toward him.

"Who stole a **Rose** from my **Garten**?" exploded

the **Bestie**. "**Bitte**, [Sir]!" said the **Papa**. → **Herr**

9

"**Bitte**, don't hurt me, **Herr**. I promised my **Tochter** that I'd bring her a **Rose** as a **Geschenk** after my long **Reise**. It was just ONE **Rose** from your **Garten**!" "It's still

stealing!" said the **Bestie**. "I will spare your life if you bring me the **Tochter** you speak of by ⎡noon⎤ in ⎡six⎤ days. Here she will live the rest of her life." Naturally, the

Mittag

sechs

Papa was very *traurig* by this request, but he promised to return with Belle at **Mittag** in **sechs** days. As he arrived at his *Haus*, each **Tochter** rushed out to greet him. He gave them each

12

the **Geschenk** they'd asked for. Each **Tochter** was very *glücklich* and shouted, "*Danke* **sehr**, *Papa!*" "*Gern geschehen!*" he replied. But he was still *traurig* because he had to tell Belle

13

ich liebe dich ←

about the promise he'd made with the **Bestie**. "Belle, I love you . **Ich liebe dich sehr** and want you to be *glücklich*. But I must tell you what I have done..." Her *Papa* went on to

14

explain what had happened that day and about the promise he had made. He warned her about how ugly the **Bestie** was, but Belle felt responsible because the **Rose** was a **Geschenk**

häßlich

she'd requested. So she agreed to go. **Sechs** days passed quickly and it was time to leave. Her sisters were very *traurig* to say *auf Wiedersehen* to Belle but they understood that she had no choice.

So Belle and her **Papa** mounted the **Pferd** and rode off. They arrived at exactly **Mittag** as instructed. Belle and her **Papa** got off the **Pferd** and approached the **Haus** of the **Bestie**.

17

Guten Tag ←

The **Tür** opened slowly and they walked in. "Hello!" said the **Papa**. "**Guten Tag**!" But there was no answer. As they walked in, they saw a **Tisch** in the middle of the **Küche** filled with food.

It looked like someone was having a **_Fest_**! Just then they heard a deep voice say, "**Guten Tag**. This ⟨lunch⟩ is especially for you. **Bitte**, enjoy!" Not wanting to be impolite, they began eating

Mittagessen

19

the magnificent **Mittagessen** before them.
And so many desserts! Belle was so excited
vier ← and already busily counting them. "...four,
fünf ← five, **sechs**. **Sechs** different, wonderful desserts!

She counted them again just to make sure, "**Eins**, **zwei**, **drei**, **vier**, **fünf**, **sechs**! It was true! **Sechs** delicious desserts all for them! They had never seen a more wonderful

Mittagessen in their lives! Suddenly, they heard footsteps approaching. There he was – the **Bestie** himself. Indeed, he was truly **häßlich**. Scared, Belle said, "**Guten Tag**,

Herr and ***danke sehr*** for the delicious

Mittagessen." "***Gern geschehen***," replied the

Bestie. He seemed very kind toward Belle. → **nett**

Her ***Papa*** was permitted to come visit her every

week which made her very *glücklich*. He gave Belle a kiss on the cheek, mounted his **Pferd**, and said, "*Auf Wiedersehen*, Belle. **Ich liebe dich sehr**, my **Tochter**!" and rode off back to his

Haus. At that **Moment**, the **Bestie** turned toward
Belle and said, "**Bitte**. What's mine is yours.
I will return every day at **Mittag** to see you."
He then quickly ran off, leaving Belle alone.

25

Because he was so **nett** toward her, Belle was no longer afraid, and was even *glücklich* when he came to visit at **Mittag**. Every day, they laughed more and more

and enjoyed sharing stories with each other. But one day, the **Bestie** didn't arrive at **Mittag** as usual. So, Belle went to look for him. She walked outside into the

Garten and there he was lying on the ground lifeless. Belle cried, "Oh, why did you have to die? **Ich liebe dich**! **Ich liebe dich sehr**!" She gave him a kiss on the cheek and suddenly,

right before her eyes, he awoke and was transformed into a **Prinz** who was very **stattlich**, indeed! He explained to her that a **böse** magician had changed him into a **Bestie** and only the kiss

of a **Mädchen** who was *verliebt* with him, and the words "**Ich liebe dich**," could change him back. The next day at **Mittag**, Belle became his *Frau*, and they all lived happily ever after.